# AN INVESTMENT JOURNEY II

## THE ESSENTIAL TOOL KIT

*Building A Successful Portfolio With Stock Fundamentals*

# Frederick A. Wilhelm Jr.

Charleston, SC
www.PalmettoPublishing.com

*AN INVESTMENT JOURNEY II: The Essential Tool Kit*
Copyright © 2022 by Frederick A. Wilhelm Jr.



Paperback ISBN: 979-8-8229-0361-6
eBook ISBN: 979-8-8229-0362-3

# ABOUT THE AUTHOR

Frederick A. Wilhelm Jr is a graduate of the U.S. Naval Academy. After serving as a fighter pilot, he received a master's degree in computer science and holds multiple patents in computer engineering.

He led the network-interconnect design team for the precursor of the internet, the ARPAnet, working with the Defense Advanced Research Projects Agency (DARPA).

His team partnered with the biotech and pharmaceutical industries and leading university artificial Intelligence (AI) departments, applying computing to DNA analysis, gene splicing, and molecular modeling applications.

Retiring from the computer industry, Fred received the CFP certificate from the College for Financial Planning.

For over 25 years, he has worked in the wealth management industry, being the former founder and CEO of Tecumseh Investment Management.

He is currently a founder and chief financial officer for the non-profit Santa Cruz Foundation for the Performing Arts.

# DISCLAIMER

The information contained within this document is for educational and entertainment purposes only. All effort has been made to present accurate, up-to-date, reliable, and complete information.

No warranties of any kind are declared or implied. Readers acknowledge that the author does not render legal, financial, medical, or professional advice. The content of this book has been derived from various sources.

Please consult a licensed professional before attempting any techniques outlined in this book.

By reading this document, the reader agrees that under no circumstances is the author responsible for any direct or indirect losses incurred as a result of the use of the information contained within this document, including, but not limited to, errors, omissions, or inaccuracies.

# PREFACE

This book is a companion to a previous publication: "AN INVESTMENT JOURNEY" by the same author.

The purpose of the two books is to provide you with the essential information and tools needed to give you the confidence to become financially independent through investing wisely; to build a solid financial foundation that will provide you with the financial freedom to last your lifetime.

This book explores many fundamental factors every investor needs to know to become more informed about the stock market in order to reduce risk and assure a successful outcome.

# TABLE OF CONTENTS
*"Scientia Est Vis"* (from knowledge-strength")

# CHAPTER ONE

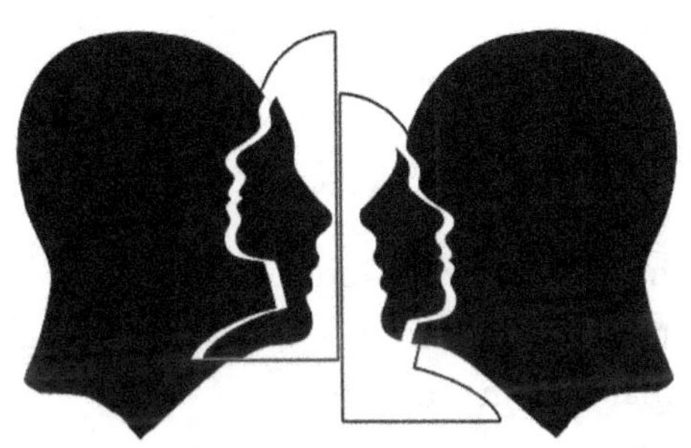

# KNOW YOURSELF

Self-evaluation concerning investing was covered exten-sively in a previous publication.

"An Investment Journey - Exploring the science and art of investing."

## Key Takeaways in that book include

- Evaluating your financial situation

- Determining your risk tolerance

- Helping you know the difference between risk tol-erance vs. risk capacity

- Making you aware of the difference between general and domain-specific risk

- Finally, learning how to quantify your level of investment risk

We all have predispositions that bias our outlook on many aspects of life, but we need to be as objective as possible when making financial decisions. This book is about how to get the most relevant information concerning any company in which you decide to become a shareholder.

# CHAPTER TWO

# FORMING YOUR STRATEGY

An investment strategy is a set of principles that guide investment decisions. Before you set your strategy, you need to assess your financial situation. Then, only invest what you are willing to risk losing.

> *There will be bear markets in the future, possibly twice every decade, so it is imperative to provide for an income stream in addition to stock investments for your retirement.*

Next, determine your goals. For example, are you investing for short-term needs like buying a car or a house, or are your goals long-term for retirement?

Clarifying your goals will help you set a strategy, as different investments have varying liquidity, opportunity, and risk levels.

Then, determine your risk tolerance. Consider age, income, and how long you have to retire. Younger investors have time to recover from losses. so they can take on more risk.

Risk is inherent in investing, with higher-risk investments often producing higher returns, while lower-risk investments are more likely to preserve their value with less upside potential.

At this point, I will refer you once again to my previous publication, "An Investment Journey," available on Amazon and Barnes & Noble.

It explicitly covers different strategies: Value investing, Growth investing, and Momentum investing.

*The best investment strategy is the one that helps you achieve your financial goals.*

# CHAPTER THREE

# KNOW THE FUNDAMENTALS

*"A Company's Bio"*

Fundamental analysis is evaluating a security to make forecasts about its future price. It typically includes reviewing many elements related to a stock, including

- Performance of the overall industry the company participates in

- Political conditions

- The company's press releases

- News releases related to the company and its business

- Competitor analysis

- Financial condition

The first step is to examine a company's publicly available information through its financial statements.

## Income Statement

The top line refers to a company's revenues or gross sales. It shows how effectively a company generates sales and revenue.

The bottom line is a company's net income. It is the income after all expenses have been deducted from revenue, which includes interest charges paid on loans, general and administrative costs, and income taxes.

A company's bottom line can also be referred to as net earnings or net profits. The earnings can be used in several ways: paying dividends to stockholders, repurchasing stock, retiring equity, spending on product development or location expansion, and other ways to improve the company.

Knowing the factors that impact both the top and bottom lines can help you determine whether a company's management is growing its sales and revenue and managing expenses efficiently.

When someone refers to profit margin, it is obtained by dividing profit by revenue. So, for example, if a company's revenue was $2.4 million and its profit was $1.2 million, its profit margin would be 50%.

## Cash Flow

Cash flows refer to the net amount of cash equivalents transferred in and out of a company. Cash received represents inflows, while money spent represents outflows.

The cash flow statement is a financial statement that reports on a company's source and usage of money over time. The cash flow statement acts as a corporate checkbook that reconciles the income statement and the balance sheet.

There are three categories of cash flows: from operations, investments, and financing.

- Operating cash flows are generated from the normal operations of a business, including money taken in from sales and money spent on the cost of goods sold, along with other operational expenses such as overhead and salaries.

- Cash flows from investments include money spent on purchasing securities to be held as investments, such as stocks or bonds in other companies or treasuries. Inflows are generated by interest and dividends paid on these holdings.

- Cash flows from financing are the transactions involving capital, such as shares or bonds the company issues or any loans it takes out. It also includes the repurchase of stock or repayment of debt.

Free cash flow (FCF) is the cash left over after a company pays for its operating expenses and CapEx (capital expenditures such as on production facilities). Companies are free to use FCF as they please.

FCF is significant since it shows how efficiently a company generates cash. A positive cash flow means more money is coming in, while a negative cash flow indicates higher spending. The latter could be a problem of excessive expense, or it could be okay because the company is investing in growth.

The cash flow statement complements the income statement and balance sheet and is a mandatory part of a company's financial reporting requirements.

## Balance Sheet

The balance sheet is an essential financial statement that should be interpreted when considering an investment in a company. It reflects the assets owned and the liabilities owed by a company at a certain point in time.

Investors can use the balance sheet to better understand a company's significant liabilities relative to its assets and if the company is financially stable enough to continue its current growth trajectory, service its debt, and expand.

An asset is anything a company owns that has value. Current assets could be converted into cash within 12 months and include things like inventory and accounts receivable. Non-current assets are long-term holdings that will generally not be converted into cash in 12 months, such as land, equipment, or intellectual property.

A liability is anything a company might owe another entity or person. Current liabilities, such as accounts payable or wages, are due within the next 12 months. Non-current liabilities are not payable within one year, such as loans, leases, or other long-term obligations.

Net worth or shareholders equity is how much the company is valued after its liabilities have been subtracted from its assets.

$$\text{Net Worth} = \text{Assets} - \text{Liabilities}$$

While a balance sheet is useful, it has some limitations. Balance sheets often record assets at their historical value rather than current value. While balance sheets account for depreciation, recorded depreciation might not account precisely for how much an asset has decreased in value.

## EBITDA
### What is it?
EBITDA is an acronym for earnings before interest, taxes, depreciation, and amortization.

With this formula, you can project a company's long-term profitability and gauge its ability to repay future financing charges.

### How is it used?
EBITDA is a handy tool for normalizing a company's results so you can more easily evaluate the business. However, it is not a substitute for other metrics, such as net income.

After all, the items excluded from EBITDA - interest, taxes, and non-cash expenses are still actual items with financial implications that should be considered.

EBITDA can also be used to generate comparisons between companies and industries.

Calculating it can help determine a company's financial health. For example, if the EBITDA is negative, it has poor cash flow.

Still, a positive EBITDA doesn't automatically mean a business has high profitability.

Nevertheless, Advocates say it provides a fairer view of how well a business performs. Moreover, for some companies, EBITDA provides a clearer picture of their long-term potential.

Tech start-ups prefer that EBITDA exclude the up-front expense of developing sophisticated software.

## Calculating EBITDA

It is relatively simple to calculate.

Start with a company's annual SEC Form 10-k or quarterly 10-Q report filed with the U.S. Securities and Exchange Commission.

Go to the operating statement, and you will find the line items for all the components in EBITDA.

Your first option for calculating it is to take the net income, interest expenses, taxes, depreciation, and amortization figures found on the income statement and add them together. The second option is to add the operating income, depreciation, and amortization figures from the income statement to find the EBITDA.

Many sites have already performed this calculation when you look up information about a stock.

## EBITDA can be deceptive

Critics say companies can use it to obscure warning signs, such as high levels of debt, escalating expenses, and lack of profitability.

Therefore EBITDA should not be used exclusively as a measure of a company's financial performance. Instead, it should only be considered as another implement among many in your fundamental analysis tool kit.

# CHAPTER FOUR

# THE ECONOMY AND THE STOCK MARKET

**"I**t's the economy, stupid!" This slogan from Bill Clinton's 1992 presidential campaign acknowledges the importance of the U.S. economy in American politics.

This slogan might also resonate loudly on Wall Street and among investors worldwide. In many ways, the economy's performance influences the stock market's success and vice versa.

The stock market and the economy are often spoken of in the same breath but are not the same, even though they usually move in tandem over the long run.

The stock market can be an indicator of how the economy is performing, but it is just one indicator.

The Gross Domestic Product or GDP measures everything the U.S. economy produces. It tracks the economy's health and represents the total dollar value of all goods and services produced over a specific period.

The marks of a good economy are strong employment numbers, higher wages, increased retail and home sales, low inflation, and consumer spending.

An increase in GDP from one period to the next should also increase the level of the stock market because consumers generally have more purchasing power and would likely devote more income toward stock market investing. In this regard, GDP is a proxy for investors' purchasing power ability.

The stock market is very different. It impacts the economy because it influences consumer confidence, which in turn affects the overall economy. The relationship also works in reverse, in that the economic conditions often impact the stock markets.

When the economy is strong, companies grow and make money. As a result, people are more likely to invest because they think profits will keep rising and companies can pay higher dividends.

Conversely, when the economy turns for the worse, people will invest less or even sell stocks.

## Stages of the Economic Cycle

The economic or business cycle is characterized by alternating periods of expansion and contraction i.e., fluctuations in economic activity.

An awareness of the characteristics of each stage of the economic cycle is critical because it serves as the starting point for top-down financial analysis.

The real gross domestic product (GDP) and the unemployment rate are the two most important economic indicators related to the economic cycle. These two indicators are used to identify at which stage of the cycle the economy is in.

There are four stages in the economic cycle:

Expansion (real GDP is increasing)

Peak (real GDP stops increasing and begins decreasing),

Contraction or recession (real GDP is decreasing),

Trough (real GDP stops decreasing and starts increasing).

The four stages of the economic cycle are illustrated in the diagram.

# THE ECONOMIC CYCLE

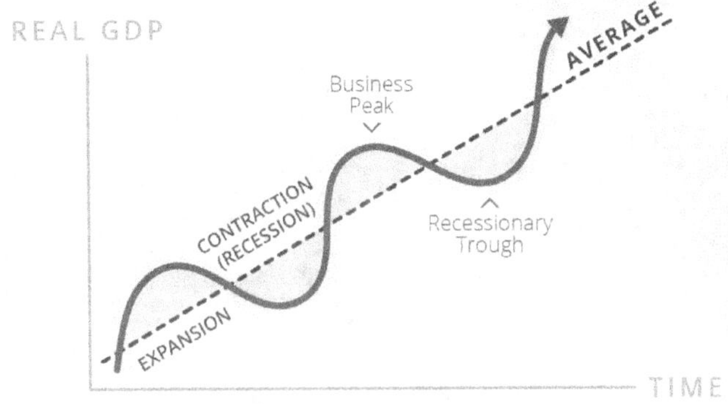


An expansion features growth in most sectors of the economy, with increasing employment, consumer spending, and business investment.

As an expansionary stage approaches its peak, the rates of increase in spending, investment, and employment slow but remain positive while inflation accelerates.

A contraction is associated with declines in most sectors. When the contraction reaches a trough, and the economy begins a new expansion or recovery, economic growth becomes positive again, and inflation is usually moderate.

A generally accepted rule is that two consecutive quarters of growth in real GDP are the beginning of an expansion, and two successive quarters of declining real GDP indicate the start of a contraction and a possible recession.

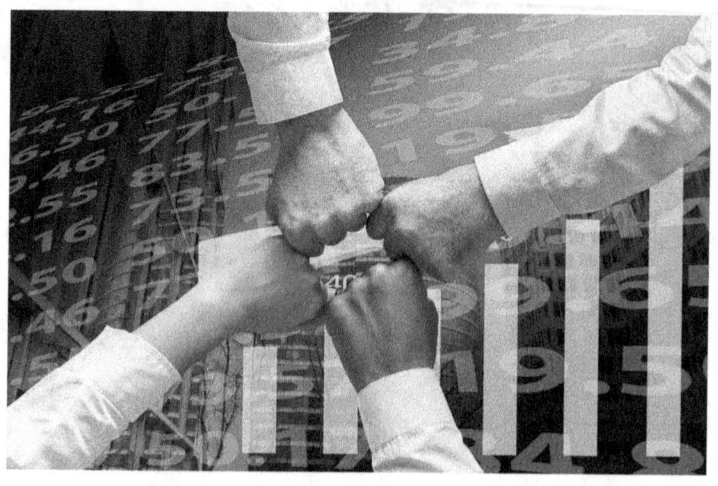

# FORCES THAT MOVE STOCKS

## Supply and Demand

The overarching force is supply and demand. When supply meets demand, there is a balance. However, any imbalance may result in a bloated inventory and lower prices for goods. As a result, a company's top-line revenue may increase while it sells more units at a lower price, but bottom-line earnings will suffer because the profit on each unit is lower.

When demand is high, and there are supply chain issues, inflation can become a severe problem.

## Disruptors

Two major disruptors have occurred concerning supply and demand: The 2020 COV ID-19 pandemic and the 2022 Ukraine-Russia war.

## The Pandemic

Over the years, we have limited manufacturing capacity in the United States because we have relied on cheap labor in other countries. So when the pandemic broke out in March 2020, supply from China, Vietnam, and others was suddenly disrupted, resulting in many shortgages of goods from overseas.

I refer to that situation as the "toilet paper crisis." Supermarket shelves became bare as people panicked and started hoarding. Suddenly supply was severely limited while demand actually increased.

The obvious result was price inflation. Business schools would define the situation as runaway price elasticity, i.e., charging what the traffic will bear. Worse than that, some goods couldn't be had at any price.

## The Ukraine-Russia War (2022)

Compounding that situation, Russia invaded Ukraine, a significant bread basket for the world. The disruption in wheat production and shipping especially impacted third-world countries.

Another effect of the war was an energy crisis in Europe caused by a gas supply disruption from Russia just as winter was coming. This disruption was principally due to an embargo on purchasing Russian gas to deny Russia one of the main sources of income to fund the war.

The United States started shipping liquid natural gas (LNG) to Europe in order to ease the situation. But, Europe did not have the infrastructure to store and distribute LNG, having relied strictly on Russian sources and pipelines. The sum total caused a spike in worldwide inflation, especially in energy prices.

## Inflation

If inflation becomes severe, wages will increase in some essential businesses, but some companies will lay off workers instead. In addition, shelter (housing and rent) will overheat initially, but as the cost of mortgages increase, housing sales will slow, and home prices will decrease.

The Federal Reserve will begin raising interest rates to cool down the economy. High-interest rates can sometimes cause a recession or stagflation (recession-inflation), a situation in which the inflation rate is high or increasing, and unemployment remains steadily high, resulting in a stagnant demand in the economy.

The negative impact of rising inflation keeps the Fed diligent and focused on detecting early warning signs to anticipate any rise. But, sometimes, they don't get it right because they usually are looking in the rearview mirror at the data.

Research suggests that value stocks are preferred by investors when inflation is high. Value stocks are shares with higher intrinsic value than their current trading price. They are frequently shares of mature, well-established companies with strong existing cash flows. During periods of high inflation, shares associated with significant current cash flows are more sought after than growth stocks that promise distant returns.

When discounting growth stocks to a present value with expected cash flows still some time ahead, the higher compounded discount rate due to inflation will adversely impact their current share price.

## Other Forces

There are also other forces not directly related to the fundamentals of a stock:

- A prominent company that experiences terrible news can affect another company's stock in the same sector. For example, a sudden negative outlook for one technology stock often hurts other technology stocks. "Guilt by association" can drag down demand for the whole sector.

- On the other hand, good earnings reports can affect the whole market mood, resulting in the entire market moving sharply upward.

- Often, stocks moving in a short-term trend can gather momentum, thus buoying their stock price even higher.

- Large-cap stocks have high liquidity because they are heavily traded, while small-cap stocks can suffer from an almost permanent liquidity discount due to low visibility.

- News related to a specific company can have positive and negative effects. For example, it could be an earnings report or future company guidance concerning plans and the company's financial outlook.

- Market sentiment refers to the psychology of market participants. For example, you may have solidly researched the fundamentals of a stock, but the market has focused on one bit of negative news, ignored the fundamentals, and as a result, your stock suffers.

*The critical thing to remember is that a company's fundamentals are the crucial bellwether over the long run. It takes discipline to ignore the day-to-day machinations of the stock market.*

# MARKET AND STOCK VOLATILITY

## The VIX

The Chicago Board Options Exchange Volatility Index, or the "VIX," as it is better known, is a measure of the expected volatility of the U.S. stock market.

The VIX is based on the option price of the S&P 500 index and is calculated by combining the weighted prices of the index's put and call options over the next 30 days.

The VIX is designed to reflect investors' view of future U.S. stock market volatility, i.e., how much investors think the S&P 500 index will fluctuate in the next 30 days.

The VIX is often referred to as the market's "fear gauge" and is used by investors to measure market risk, fear and stress before they make an investment decision.

The greater the perceived market risk, the more they are willing to pay for "insurance" in the form of options. Hedging this way involves an investor taking an opposite position in a stock to the one they hold by buying an option.

The higher the VIX, the higher the fear, which according to market contrarians, is considered a buy signal. But, of course, the reverse is true—the lower the VIX, the lower the fear, which indicates a more complacent market.

In general, VIX values of greater than 30 are considered to signal heightened volatility from increased uncertainty, risk and investor fear. Conversely, a VIX below 20 generally corresponds to more stable, less stressful periods in the market.

## Stock Volatility

Beta measures the volatility of a security or portfolio compared to the market.

Beta data about an individual stock can give an investor an approximation of how much risk the stock will add to a diversified portfolio. For example, the S&P 500 has a beta of 1.0.

A beta greater than 1.0 indicates that the security's price is theoretically more volatile than the market. For example, if a stock's beta is 1.2, it is assumed to be 20%

more volatile than the market. Technology and small-cap stocks tend to have higher betas, indicating that adding these stocks to a portfolio will increase risk but may also increase its expected return.

The beta coefficient assumes that stock returns are normally distributed from a statistical perspective. However, financial markets are prone to surprises, so, in reality, returns are only sometimes normally distributed.

Therefore, what a stock's beta might predict about its future movement isn't always true.

Practical use of beta will depend on your risk tolerance and goals. For example, if you want to replicate the broader market average in your portfolio, an S & P 500 index exchange-traded fund (ETF) with a beta of 1.0 is ideal.

On the other hand, if you are a very conservative investor looking to preserve principal, a low beta may be more appropriate. In a bull market, a beta greater than 1.0 will tend to produce above-average returns and more significant losses in a down market.

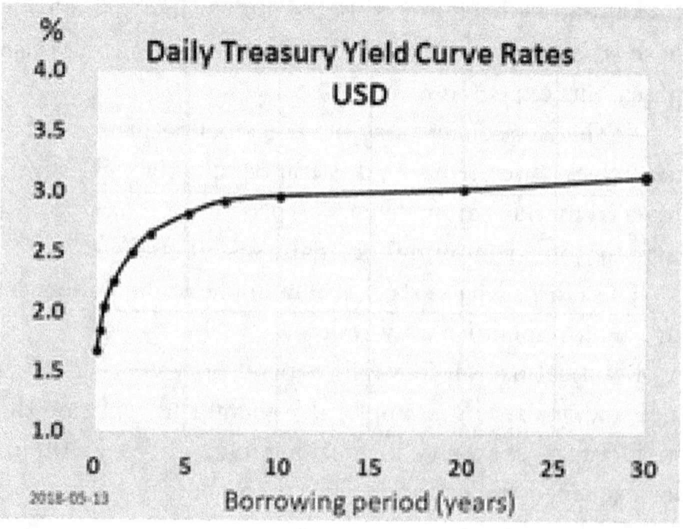


# INTEREST RATES AND EFFECT ON STOCKS

## Rates

The short-term interest rate set by the central bank (Federal Reserve) dramatically affects economic growth, inflation, the housing market, equity valuations, bond valuations, and even gold prices.

The Fed lowers this key rate when it wants to produce "easy money" to stimulate the economy. A low-interest rate for all types of debt encourages consumers and businesses to borrow money and use it to consume or expand, which benefits the economy in the short term.

In contrast, the Fed increases this rate when it wants to tighten money to reduce or prevent price inflation, to deflate economic bubbles (demand destruction), or to improve the desirability of holding its currency compared to other currencies.

Raising rates makes saving money in bank accounts more appealing and borrowing capital for consumption or business expansion less attractive.

Generally speaking, the Fed reduces interest rates shortly before or during recessions and then starts raising interest rates after the economic recovery when inflation starts to rise. Likewise, when interest rates rise, high-quality bonds with yields well above an inflation rate look more attractive.

## Follow the money - The stock-bond relationship

Bonds are debt-based investments issued by governments and companies when they need to raise additional capital. In return for loaning money, investors receive regular interest repayments (called coupons) and get their capital back at a specified time in the future (called the maturity date).

Stocks and bonds compete for the finite quantity of investor funds. As a result, bonds would be considered the safer investment, while stocks usually offer more significant profit opportunities. This relationship creates an environment where investors favor one over the other in order to rebalance their portfolio, particularly in times of positive or negative economic growth.

Investors are incentivized to move out of stocks and into bonds as bond interest rates increase. As a result, falling demand for stocks has a negative impact on their prices. In addition, as interest rates rise, it costs companies more to borrow, increasing costs and lowering profits, thus putting additional pressure on stock prices.

In summary, Stocks and bonds compete for investors' funds and usually have an inverse relationship in value. Therefore, lower bond yields could lead to higher share prices, and higher bond yields could lead to lower share prices.

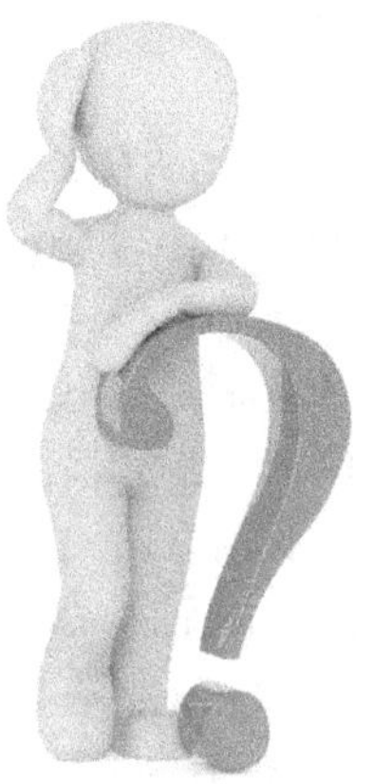

# CHAPTER EIGHT

# STOCK RESEARCH

## Key steps to evaluate any stock

Start by reviewing the company's financials, called quantitative research. It begins with gathering a few documents that companies are required to file with the U.S. Securities and Exchange Commission (SEC)

- **Form 10-K:** An annual report that includes financial statements that have been independently audited. Here you can review a company's balance sheet, its sources of income, and how it handles its cash, revenues, and expenses.

- **Form 10-Q:** A quarterly update on operations and financial results.

## Best stock research websites

The SEC's Electronic Data Gathering Analysis and Retrieval (EDGAR) website provides a searchable database of the forms named above. It's a valuable resource for learning how to research stocks.

Short on time? You'll find highlights from the above filings and important financial ratios on your brokerage firm's website or major financial news websites. This information will help you compare a company's performance against other candidates competing for your investment dollars.

## Narrow your focus

Financial reports contain many numbers. Focus on the following line items to become familiar with the measurable inner workings of a company:

## Revenue

It is the amount of money a company brings in during a specified period. It's the first thing you'll see on the income statement, which is why it's often referred to as the "top line."

Sometimes revenue is broken down into "operating revenue" and "nonoperating revenue." Operating revenue is most telling because it's generated from the company's core business.

Nonoperating revenue often comes from one-time business activities like selling an asset.

## Net income

This "bottom line" figure is the total amount of money a company has made after operating expenses, taxes, and depreciation are subtracted from revenue.

Revenue is the equivalent of your gross salary, and net income is comparable to what's left over after you've paid taxes and living expenses.

## Earnings and earnings per share (EPS)

When you divide earnings by the number of shares available to trade, you get earnings per share. This number shows a company's profitability on a per-share basis, which makes it easier to compare with other companies.

When you see earnings per share followed by "(ttm)" that refers to the trailing twelve months.

Earnings are far from a perfect financial measurement because it doesn't tell you how or how efficiently the company uses its capital. For example, some companies take those earnings and reinvest them in the business. Others pay them out to shareholders in the form of dividends.

## P/E Ratio

We can go a step further to perform some fundamental valuations on companies by analyzing the P/E Ratio/ It is derived by dividing the price of a stock share by its earnings per share (EPS).

If a company's stock trades at $100 per share and generates $4 per share in annual earnings, the P/E ratio would be 25 (100/4). Given the company's current profits, it would take 25 years of accumulated earnings to equal the investment cost. The ratio changes as companies report earnings, typically every quarter.

The higher the ratio, the more expensive a stock is relative to its earnings. The lower the ratio, the less expensive. In this way, stocks can be classified as growth or value investments. An investment with an above-average ratio would be considered a growth investment, while a company with a below-average ratio would be regarded as a value investment. Technology companies with expectations of future high growth prospects would have a high P/E ratio.

The modern-era market average is 19.6. However, the year 2020 average, for example, was 28.6, 41 % above the average, suggesting that the market was overvalued.

## Price-to-Book Ratio

The price-to-book (P/B) ratio is a financial ratio that shows how much the stock is worth compared to the company's book value. It is computed by taking the price per share and dividing that by the book value per share.

For example, if a company worth $10 million has 500,000 shares outstanding, it will have a book value per share of:

$10,000,000 / 500,000 shares = $20 book value per share

If its stock trades at $80 per share, then the P/B ratio is:

$80 / $20 = 4 P/B ratio

If the P/B ratio is more than 1, the market's consensus is that the stock will grow at a faster pace than its book value suggests, which is why its price is higher than its book value. In some cases, you can see very high P/B ratios of 100 or more. High P/B ratios are often seen in high-growth stocks.

## Return on Equity (ROE)

The return on equity is a measurement that determines how efficiently a company uses its shareholders' equity. You calculate the ROE by dividing the shareholders' equity by the company's net income. If a company has generated $5 million this year and its shareholder's equity is $50 million, this means the ROE is:

$$\$5,000,000 \, / \, \$50,000,000 = 0.1 \text{ or } 10\%$$

Note that analysts typically display the ROE result as a percentage. The higher the ROE, the more efficient the company is. If a company generates a less than $5 million income this year (say $2 million) with the same shareholders' equity, this means it is less efficient:

$$\$2,000,000 \, / \, \$50,000,000 = 0.04 \text{ or } 4\%$$

Here, the company has a lower ROE given the same shareholder's equity, so it is less efficient in using its shareholders' equity to generate income.

## ROA Formula / Return on Assets Calculation

Return on Assets (ROA) is a type of metric that measures the profitability of a business in relation to its total assets. This ratio indicates how well a company performs by comparing the profit (net income) it generates to the capital it invests in assets. The higher the return, the more productive and efficient management is in utilizing economic resources. The ROA formula is

ROA = Net Income / Average Assets

or

ROA = Net Income / End of Period Assets

Where:

Net income is equal to net earnings or net income in the year (annual period)

Average Assets is equal to ending assets minus beginning assets divided by 2

Typically, different industries have different ROAs. Industries that are capital-intensive and require a high value of fixed assets for operations will generally have a lower ROA, as their large asset base will increase the denominator of the formula. Naturally, a company with a large asset base can have a large ROA if its income is high enough..

ROA is important because it makes companies more easily comparable. Imagine two companies… one with a net income of $50 million and assets of $500 million, the other with a net income of $10 million and assets of $15 million. The first company earns a return on assets of 10% and the second one earns a ROA of 67%.

Return on assets indicates the amount of money earned per dollar of assets. Therefore, a higher return on assets value indicates that the second business is more profitable and efficient.

It is important to note that return on assets should not be compared across industries. Companies in different industries vary significantly in their use of assets. For example, some industries may require expensive property, plant, and equipment to generate income as opposed to companies in other industries.

Therefore, these companies would naturally report a lower return on assets when compared to companies that do not require a lot of assets to operate. Therefore, return on assets should only be used to compare with companies within an industry.

Return on assets can be used to gauge how asset-intensive a company is:

- The lower the return on assets, the more asset-intensive a company is. An example of an asset-intensive company would be an airline company.

- The higher the return on assets, the less asset-intensive a company is. An example of an asset-light company would be a software company.

As a general rule, a return on assets under 5% is considered an asset-intensive business, while a return on assets above 20% is considered an asset-light business.

## How does the company make money?

Sometimes it's obvious, such as a clothing retailer whose primary business is selling clothes. Sometimes it's not, such as a fast-food company that derives most of its revenue from selling franchises or an electronics firm that relies on providing consumer financing for growth.

## Does the company have a competitive advantage?

Look for something about the business that makes it difficult to imitate, equal, or eclipse. It could be its brand, business model, ability to innovate, research capabilities, patent ownership, operational excellence, or superior distribution capabilities. These competitive advantages are sometimes called the company's moat.

The harder it is for competitors to breach the company's moat, the stronger the competitive advantage.

## How good is the management team?

A company is only as good as its leaders' ability to plot a course and steer the enterprise. You can find out a lot about management by reading their words in the transcripts of company conference calls and annual reports.

Also, research the company's board of directors, who are the people representing shareholders in the boardroom. Be wary of boards composed mainly of company insiders. You want to see a healthy number of independent thinkers who can objectively assess management's actions.

## Finally, put your stock research into context.

There are endless metrics and ratios investors can use to evaluate a company's general financial health and calculate the intrinsic value of its stock.

But looking solely at a company's revenue or income from a single year or the management team's most recent decisions paints an incomplete picture.

Before you buy any stock, you want to build a well-informed narrative about the company and what factors make it worthy of a long-term partnership. And to do that, context is key.

For long-term context, pull back the lens of your research to look at historical data. It will give you insight into the company's resilience during tough times, reactions to challenges, and ability to improve its performance and deliver shareholder value over time.

Then look at how the company fits into the big picture by comparing the numbers and key ratios to industry averages and other companies in the same or similar business.

Many brokers offer research tools on their websites. The easiest way to make these comparisons is by using your broker's educational tools, such as a stock screener. In addition, there are several free stock screeners available online.

## The bottom line on how to research stocks

Stock research is as simple as

- gathering materials from the right websites

- looking at some key numbers (quantitative stock research)

- asking some critical questions (qualitative stock research), and

- looking at how a company compares to its industry peers, as well as how it compares to itself in years past.

# CHAPTER NINE

# PART I – MARKET WARNING SIGNS

## Prolonged Dovish Monetary Policy

The United States Federal Reserve Bank, also called the Fed, is the central bank of the U.S., meaning the bank is charged with determining monetary policy for the U.S.

## Fed Funds Rate

The fed funds rate is the interest rate charged between banks to lend excess funds overnight. When this rate is lower, interest rates on loans like mortgages, auto loans, and credit cards become lower, spurring a wave of lending.

Of course, when consumers can borrow more money relatively cheaply, they tend to do so, creating tons of liquidity in the U.S. economy.

As a result, spending ensues, leading to higher revenues and profitability for corporations and, ultimately, a bull market.

However, prolonged low rates can be a warning sign because they can't last forever. At some point, debt will have to slow, and rates will have to increase, resulting in a tightening of consumer spending and, if the contraction is significant, a possible recession leading to a bear market.

## Bond Buying Programs

Another way the Fed works to stimulate growth in the economy is to buy bonds. By purchasing massive numbers of bonds, the Fed exchanges liquid cash today for bonds with future maturity dates. This liquidity floods the market with spendable money and leads to the same loose spending that low rates often encourage.

But, like with low rates, the party doesn't last forever. At some point, the bonds purchased will mature, but the Fed will likely slow its bond-buying activities even before that.

As this happens, many businesses expect reduced revenues because consumers tend to spend less, potentially resulting in a down market.

## A Bubble In Market Valuations

Bubbles always appear in the stock market. History's most memorable include the:

## Dot.com Bubble

During the late 90s, the excitement around the widespread adoption of the Internet ran high. As a result, stocks representing virtually any online company rocketed, leading to outlandishly high valuations in the sector.

With investors earning such massive returns, nobody seemed to be paying attention to the excessively high prices they were paying to own slivers of companies that, in many cases, weren't making a dime.

When the bubble popped, the entire market took a hit.

## The Real Estate Bubble

Following the dot-com bubble burst, excessive monetary stimulus and poor lending practices led to a flood of demand for real estate, sending property prices skyrocketing. When the real estate bubble popped in 2007, a massive sell-off began, and the Great Recession set in.

After the Great Recession, the stock market enjoyed the longest bull run in history, climbing for more than ten years before COVID-19 took its toll.

## An Extended Bull Market

The market is thought to be a balanced system, but the reality is that it's anything but balanced. From day to day, month to month, and even year to year, the stock market struggles to keep valuations in check as the bears and bulls argue their points.

According to Forbes, the average bull market lasts about two years and seven months. So an uninterrupted run of the bulls that lasts considerably longer could signify that we're due for a reversal.

Any time the bulls take control for too long, the prices investors pay to own stock go through the roof, generally creating excessive overvaluations. On the other side of the coin, too much control by bears sends stock prices tumbling, resulting in extreme undervaluations.

## Corporate Profits Turn Flat

One of the key drivers in the stock market is profit. Nobody wants to invest in a company that's losing money with no sign of profitability. But conversely, investors are happy and willing to risk investing more money into stocks when profits grow.

During economic uncertainty, when consumer confidence is lacking the most, consumer spending often dries up, leading to plateaus in profitability for many businesses and widespread stock sell-offs.

## A High Cyclically Adjusted Price-to-Earnings (CAPE) Ratio

Another clear-cut warning sign that a bear market could be on the horizon is a high cyclically adjusted price-to-earnings (CAPE) ratio.

The ratio is a 10-year moving average of the traditional price-to-earnings ratio, which measures a company's profitability in relation to its share price.

The metric was developed by Robert Schiller in 1996 and has been used by stock market experts and economists for over two decades. Also called the Schiller P/E, the CAPE ratio averages price-to-earnings ratios over the past ten years, which essentially washes out short-term peaks, valleys, and volatility to show whether the market is truly under or overvalued. A healthy CAPE is in the 15 or 16 range. A CAPE can be calculated for an individual stock, an industry sector, or the market as a whole. You can even calculate it for your portfolio.

Anything over 20 is cause for concern, and when the figure nears 30, it's a clear warning sign that something big is on the horizon. If you measure the CAPE of the S&P 500 index just before the Great Depression, you'll see that it climbed as high as 33.1.

## Rising Inflation

Some inflation is natural. As the economy progresses, a slow and steady increase in prices for consumer goods, services, and any other category is normal. It's why your great-grandparents could buy an entire lunch for a dime, and today it's hard to find a stick of bubble gum for that price.

Inflation becomes a problem when it happens too fast. The U.S. Federal Reserve targets stabilized inflation at 2%, which it feels is the healthy rate at which prices should increase.

As prices rise, consumers become more fiscally conscious, often leading to increased saving activities and decreased overall spending. From there, reduced corporate profitability is on the horizon, potentially leading to a down stock market.

## The Buffett Indicator

The Buffett Indicator is a fundamental measure of whether the stock market is under or overvalued. It was first proposed in 2001 by the iconic investor Warren Buffett.

Since then, the indicator has been used by economists and Wall Street experts almost religiously. It is calculated by dividing the total market value by the gross domestic product (GDP).

(The most comprehensive view of the total U.S. markets currently is provided by the Wilshire 5000 Index - the oldest broad-based index covering the entire U.S. investable market.)

According to Buffett, the market is valued fairly when the Buffett indicator is between 75% and 90%. Once the indicator climbs to between 90% and 115%, the market is modestly overvalued. Finally, whenever the indicator is over 115%, the market is poised for significant declines.

The indicator peaked at 136.9% during the dot.com bubble in 2000. The indicator on 11/18/2022 was 164%, indicating the market was significantly overvalued.

Mkt value of 42.4 trillion divided by GDP
of 25.8 trillion = 164%

## Excessively High Market Sentiment

Emotion is a key driver of movement in the stock market.

In some cases, emotions can run extremely high, leading investors to throw fundamental analysis out the window and make emotionally driven decisions that either drive prices to extreme undervaluations or overvaluations.

One of the best ways to gauge this is using the Fear & Greed index. Developed by CNN Money, the index was designed to measure whether investors are too bullish or too bearish based on emotions that drive the market.

## Domestic and Geopolitical Uncertainty

Politics will always play a significant role in stock market activity. Legislative changes have the potential to pick up or destroy large sections of the economy, whether those political changes happen here at home or around the world.

Political uncertainty is a common concern. After all, when investors don't know what to expect, they're not willing to risk their money, leading to less investor interest and declines in market values.

On the international stage, many argue that geopolitical uncertainty will continue for some time as China, Russia, and Iran vie for power and many western countries face internal political turmoil. As a result, continued uncertainty or significant political events could weigh heavily on the market.

## Inverted Yield Curve

An inverted yield curve occurs when long-term rates on fixed-income securities fall below short-term rates. The term inverted is used to describe this action because long-term fixed-income investments usually pay a higher return than their short-term counterparts.

When the curve is inverted, it suggests that investors believe economic struggles are ahead. Historically, this has been a clear signal of a coming recession. In fact, over the past 50 years, an inverted curve occurred just before each recession, with only one inverted curve happening and not followed by a recession.

You can find the yield curve at ustreasuryyieldcurve.com for any date.

## Weakening Economic Indicators

Many investors look to the Conference Board Leading Economic Index, or LEI, which considers the following indicators, which can be found at conference-board.org.

- **Manufacturing**. When more manufacturing takes place, it's a sign that economic conditions are favorable. The LEI tracks average weekly manufacturing hours and new orders for manufactured consumer goods, materials, and nondefense capital goods, excluding aircraft orders.

- **Unemployment Claims**. When economic conditions are booming, there tend to be fewer unemployment claims; the opposite is true when economic conditions are a cause for concern.

- **Housing Market**. If economic conditions are favorable, consumers are more likely to purchase a new home. But, if there's a slowing in the housing market, including home sales, building permits, and new private housing units, there's likely a slowing in the overall economy.

- **Stock Prices**. The U.S. stock market and the state of the economy are heavily correlated. The LEI factors in the prices of stocks in the S&P 500 index to determine if the market is reacting to economic uncertainties.

- **Credit Index**. Consumers are more likely to take out new loans when they feel economic conditions will make paying those loans back relatively easy, and they are less likely to borrow when economic conditions are concerning.

  The U.S. credit index measures the performance of taxable corporate, fixed-rate, and government income securities, helping to determine the state of the economy based on returns in the fixed-income sector.

- **Treasury Bond Yields**. Finally, the LEI compares 10-year Treasury bond yields minus the fed funds rate. The difference is the premium investors are willing to pay for mid-term Treasury bonds.

## Declining Vehicle Sales

Vehicle sales are an excellent gauge of what's happening with the U.S. economy. Therefore, they can be an excellent indicator of the stock market's direction.

The purchase of a new vehicle is a big decision with a significant price tag. Most people take advantage of loans when buying cars because they can't afford to buy them comfortably with cash.

As a result, vehicle sales tend to be positive when consumers believe favorable economic conditions are ahead and seem to hit a brick wall when the overall sentiment turns negative.

By looking at vehicle sales growth, you'll gauge how consumers feel about economic conditions and their confidence in making big-ticket purchases.

## Declining Home Sales

The reason to track home sales falls along similar lines; consumers aren't as cavalier about buying a home if they don't feel comfortable with the state of the economy.

## A Black Swan Event

In a black swan event, none of the above matters. These rare, unforeseen events happen entirely out of the blue, leading to dramatic market declines. Some examples of black swan events in recent history include:

- **COVID-19**. The most recent black swan event occurred in early 2020 when COVID-19 swept the world. The virus came out of nowhere, leading to lockdowns and driving the market down tremendously in a short period of time.

- **Terrorist Attacks**. On September 11, 2001, a terrorist attack on New York City and the Pentagon shook the United States. The resulting fear of further attacks and geopolitical fallout led to significant declines in the market.

- **Soviet Union Dissolution**. The collapse of the Soviet Union took place in 1991. The geopolitical uncertainty that followed led markets to tremendous lows.

By their nature, black swan events are rare and unpredictable. There's no way to tell if a black swan event will happen tomorrow or ten years from now, but when they do, they tend to lead to market crashes.

# PART II – STOCK WARNING SIGNS

- One sign of a bad investment is a company's goals, or benchmarks get moved when they are missed, or the company repeatedly changes its strategy.

- The stock's P/E is higher than others in the same industry, and you can't explain why it's out of sync.

- Conversely, very low PE ratios should be considered investment warning signs. It may mean that the stock appears cheap based on past earnings, but future earnings could be much lower, crossing the line between investing vs. speculating.

- A company reducing the size of its dividend is a sure sign that things are not going well. If it must reduce its dividend, it means profits are under pressure, or things are not going according to plan

- Key management leaves. The new management doesn't clearly articulate the vision for company growth and profitability and is reluctant to make needed changes.

- The company is about to embark on a sizable ill-advised acquisition.

- The company itself has been acquired, and the new acquisition makes no sense.

- The company's earnings growth has drastically slowed from the previous year.

- The company consistently uses more cash than it makes.

- If a company delays or postpones the release of its financial results, it will often mean bad news is on the way. On the other hand, it may mean that the company's auditors are reluctant to sign off on the results. Either way, it is a potential early warning sign that the stock is a bad investment.

- Asset write-downs are often investment warning signs for investors. A write-down will reduce the value of the company's equity, and invariably the stock price will fall substantially.

- When a company is in trouble, communication with investors stops.

- Rising and high debt levels are investment warning signs. You can compare a company's debt-to-equity level to the rest of its sector to see what is reasonable.

- Key managers in the company start to sell a considerable amount of stock or buy put options to protect their stock if the price falls.

- The company's sales are on the decline.

*If your stock shows more than a few warning signs, you need to ask yourself why you're holding the shares.*

# THE FINAL STEP

## CREATING YOUR INVESTMENT PORTFOLIO

Following a structured approach, you can create your portfolio to align with your investment strategies. Your portfolio will be a collection of assets such as stocks, mutual funds, and exchange-traded funds. It should meet your future capital requirements.

### Goals

Remember the goals you thought of while reading this book. You might have multiple objectives, such as:

- Planning for a large purchase, a home, or a car.

- Starting a business

- Funding a child's education

- As well as saving for retirement

What is important to you? The most significant risk you face is not in the stock market - it's in reaching your goals.

## Risk tolerance

The second factor to consider is your personality and risk tolerance. Are you willing to hazard a potential loss for the possibility of greater returns?

You don't want to eliminate risk so much as optimize it for your situation and lifestyle.

For example, younger persons can take higher risks because they have more time to recover from losses, whereas older people nearing retirement need to focus on protecting assets and drawing income from them tax-efficiently.

## Allocation

There are risk and return expectations associated with each investment you choose.

A 100% fixed-income portfolio will likely have lower risk and lower returns, while an equity-only portfolio will generally have higher risk and higher returns.

# Diversification

Your next aim should be to build a diversified portfolio offering optimal returns while safeguarding your investments from undesirable eventualities, for you can never be sure of what the future holds.

A diversified portfolio could consist of several ETFs covering different sectors like industrial, healthcare, technology, food companies, real estate, etc.

This way, if one company in a sector is hit hard by the market, your other investments will ameliorate any losses.

It is not enough to simply own securities from each asset class. You must also diversify within each. Make sure your holdings within a given asset class are spread across various subclasses and industry sectors.

# Monitor Your Portfolio

After following all the above, you must track the performance of your investments.

If the portfolio is not meeting your goal expectations, you should analyze and identify the reasons. You may have to make adjustments, but only after serious thought and consideration of all the factors.

# Rebalancing

Some advisors recommend rebalancing your portfolio at set intervals, such as every 6 or 12 months, or when the allocation of one of your asset classes (such as stocks) shifts by more than a predetermined percentage, such as 5%.

For example, if you have an investment portfolio with 60% stocks and its value increases to 65%, you may want to sell some of your stocks and invest in other asset classes until your stock allocation drops back to 60%.

When rebalancing and readjusting your portfolio, take a moment to consider the tax implications of selling assets at any moment in time.

## Bottom Line

*As you craft your portfolio, keep in mind your goals and the fundamentals you studied in selecting it. Don't let the volatility and vagaries of the market sway you from your plan. A well-thought-out portfolio will give you peace of mind as it positions you firmly for building wealth.*

# FUNDAMENTAL VS. TECHNICAL ANALYSIS

There are two very different schools of thought: technicians who look only at past performance using charts in deciding to trade a stock and those who look at a company's intrinsic value using fundamental analysis. They both have their value and can be used to advantage when deciding to buy or sell a stock.

Fundamental analysts study everything from the overall economy and industry conditions to individual companies' financial strength and management. Earnings, expenses, assets, and liabilities all come under scrutiny by fundamental analysts.

Fundamental analysts try to determine a company's value by looking at its income statement, balance sheet, and cash flow statement. In financial terms, an investor tries to measure a company's intrinsic value by discounting the value of future projected cash flows to a net present value. A stock price that trades below a company's intrinsic value is typically considered a good investment opportunity and vice versa.

Investors who perform fundamental analysis rely on financial statements that are filed quarterly, as well as changes in earnings per share that do not emerge on a daily basis, like price and volume information. Part of the reason that fundamental analysts use a long-term time frame is that the data they use to analyze a stock is generated much more slowly than technical analysts' price and volume data.

Technical analysis and fundamental analysis typically have different goals in mind. Technical analysts often try to identify many short- to medium-term trades where they can flip a stock, while fundamental analysts usually try to make long-term investments in a stock's underlying business.

Technical analysts generally believe that there's no reason to analyze a company's financial statements since the stock price already includes all relevant information. Instead, the investor focuses on analyzing the stock chart itself for hints about where the price may be headed.

A chart of past performance over long or short periods can literally paint a picture. The trend lines of price, Relative strength (RSI), moving average (MA), and trading bands (Bollinger Bands) are a quick snapshot of the company.

## Relative Strength Index (RSI)

RSI is a technical indicator used in the analysis of financial markets. It is intended to chart the current and historical strengths or weaknesses of a stock or market based on the closing prices of a recent trading period.

The RSI measures the velocity and magnitude of price movements. Momentum is the rate of the rise or fall in price. The RSI computes momentum as the ratio of higher closes to overall closes: stocks with more or stronger positive changes have a higher RSI than stocks with more or stronger negative changes.

The RSI provides signals that tell investors to buy when the security is oversold and to sell when it is overbought.

## Moving Average (MA)

In finance, a moving average (MA) is a stock indicator commonly used in technical analysis. Calculating a stock's moving average is to help smooth out the price data by creating a constantly updated average price. By calculating the moving average, the impacts of random, short-term fluctuations on the price of a stock over a specified time frame are mitigated.

Moving averages are calculated to identify a stock's trend direction or determine its support and resistance levels. It is a trend-following or lagging indicator because it is based on past prices.

The longer the period for the moving average, the greater the lag. A 200-day moving average will have a much greater degree of lag than a 20-day MA because it contains prices for the past 200 days. 50-day and 200-day moving average figures are widely followed by investors and traders and are considered to be important trading signals.

Investors may choose different periods of varying lengths to calculate moving averages based on their trading objectives. Shorter moving averages are typically used for short-term trading, while longer-term moving averages are more suited for long-term investors.

While predicting a specific stock's future movement is impossible, technical analysis and research can help make better predictions. A rising moving average indicates that the security is in an uptrend, while a declining moving average indicates that it is in a downtrend

## Bollinger Bands

Flexible and visually intuitive to many traders, Bollinger Bands® can be a helpful technical analysis tool. Invented in 1983 by John Bollinger, they're designed to help traders evaluate price action and a stock's volatility.

A Bollinger Band consists of a middle band (which is a moving average) and an upper and lower band. The general principle is that by comparing a stock's position relative to the bands, a trader may be able to determine if a stock's price is relatively low or relatively high.

The width of the band can be an indicator of its volatility (narrower bands indicate less volatility, while wider ones indicate higher volatility).

Bollinger Bands typically use a 20-period moving average, where the "period" could be 5 minutes, an hour, or a day. By default, the upper and lower bands are set two standard deviations above and below the moving average. However, traders can customize the number of periods in the moving average as well as the number of deviations.

When the price touches the upper band, it doesn't necessarily mean that you should sell. Similarly, when the price touches the lower band, it doesn't necessarily mean you should buy.

Prices can "walk the band" during a strong down or uptrend. This means that there are repeated instances of a price touching or breaking through the lower or upper band. That's why you may not want to take action when the price touches either band—you might, instead, prefer to wait.

This chart is a one month display of Amazon on 12/2/2022 illustrating its Bollinger Bands.

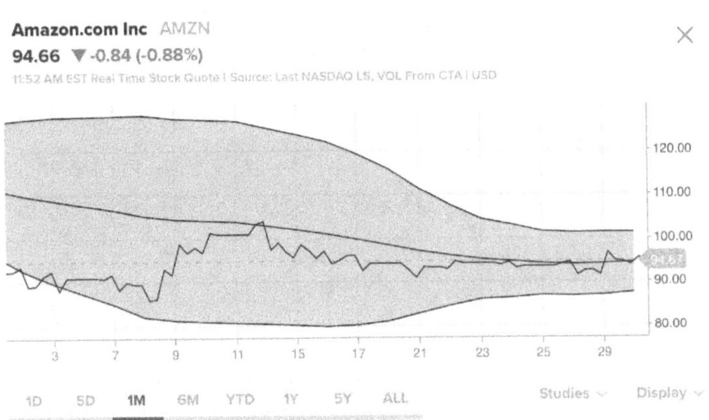

# We can compare that to Walmart

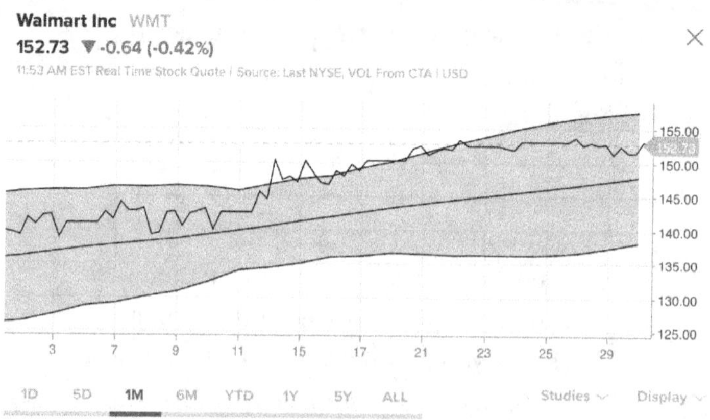

# FUNDAMENTAL ANALYSIS EXAMPLE

In this example, we are going to analyze two companies in a competing sector, Walmart and Amazon. Walmart is bricks and mortar, but moving quickly online. Past price history performance gives us some relative perspective.

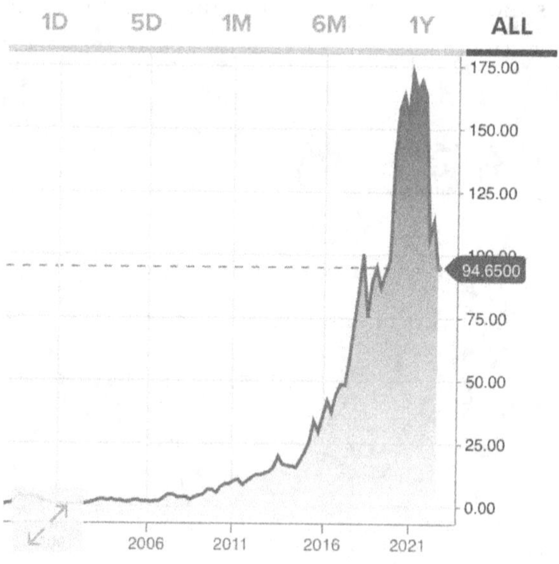


Data compiled on 12/2/2022

| Item | WMT | AMZN | ADVANTAGE |
|---|---|---|---|
| PRICE $ | 152.71 | 94.68 | |
| DIVIDEND % | 1.47 | 0 | WMT |
| REVENUE (B) | 600 | 502 | |
| NET PROFIT MARGIN % | 1.52 | 2.26 | AMZN |
| EPS $ (diluted) | 3.26 | 1.09 | WMT |
| P/E | 46.84 | 86.84 | WMT |
| P/B | 5.73 | 7 | WMT |
| ROA % | 3.7 | 2.8 | WMT |
| ROE % | 11.61 | 8.78 | WMT |
| BETA | 0.53 | 1.30 | WMT |
| RSI | 74.44 | 43.59 | WMT |
| | | | |

## Dividend

Walmart pays a dividend which would be attractive to a value investor.

## EPS and P/E Ratio

Amazon's EPS seems low compared to its stock price of 94.6. This results in an extremely high P/E ratio.

This tells us that only a small part of earnings goes to shareholders compared to Walmart. This may be because Amazon is expanding and reinvesting more heavily in its business.

## Book Value and PriceTo Book (P/B)

A company's book value equals assets minus liabilities, so:

Price-to-book ratio = share price divided by the book value per share The easiest way to get P/B is just google it.

Some analysts say a P/B ratio of less than 1 indicates a stock is undervalued, and everything else being equal may be poised for a rise.

A P/B ratio of 3 or higher could signal a market value that's too high and may be ready for a fall. P/B ratios are best used to compare companies in the same business.

Amazon's P/B ratio is quite high compared to Walmart's.

## ROE

Walmart's ROE of 11.61% suggests it is more efficient than Amazon in generating returns on shareholder investment.

## ROA

ROA shows the percentage of how profitable a company's assets are in generating revenue. The numbers show that Walmart is slightly more efficient than Amazon in this regard.

## Beta Volatility

The Beta coefficient is essentially the comparison of a particular stock to the market as a whole, represented by the S&P 500, which has a Beta equal to 1.0.

If a stock has a Beta greater than 1.0, then it has a component of what is called idiosyncratic risk. Stocks are all assumed to carry two types of risk

1. Idiosyncratic risk

2. Systemic (or market) risk:

The good news is that diversification can reduce idiosyncratic risk.

We can see that Amazon is almost three times as volatile as Walmart but only slightly higher than the S&P 500 index.

# CONCLUSION

*You would have to draw your own conclusions as there are many other factors to consider about the state of the economy, inflation, future market outlook, and especially your goals and strategy.*

# FINAL THOUGHTS

It has been my privilege to be your guide throughout this journey. Now, you are on your own and need to keep informed and updated in an ever-changing world that could affect your investments.

Be on the lookout for disrupting advancements that will provide opportunities. To keep being a winner, you have to always be on top of new developments.

At the same time, keep a cool head and your long-term goals in mind. Markets will swing wildly at times, but as long as your portfolio makes fundamental sense, stay the course.

Don't be swayed by the "experts." Instead, take that first step to achieve what you have conceived, and develop the mindset to be the winner you already are. I wish you the best.

Happy investing.

Frederick A. Wilhelm Jr.

# ACKNOWLEDGMENTS

I would like to thank my wife, Christina Wilhelm, for her knowledgeable questions and probing eyes.

Gerry Isaac's business background and thoroughness were especially invaluable.

I appreciate all the references that were of great help in writing this book, especially:

nerdwallet, investopedia, wikipedia, poweropt, moneycrashers, seekingalpha, vanguard, lynalden, lehnerinvestments, fidelity. pixabay, napkinfinance, public.com, fool.com, daily.com, forbes, edwardjones